FRAGMENTS OF PEACE
IN A WORLD AT WAR

FRAGMENTS OF PEACE
IN A WORLD AT WAR

PHOTOGRAPHS, POETRY, AND PERSPECTIVE

JOHN CANDLER (Jock) COBB MD MPH
American Field Service Ambulance Driver in World War II, 1942–1944

ANIMIST PRESS
Questa, New Mexico

First Edition

An Animist Press Book
Renny Russell, publisher
HC 81, Box 628
Questa, New Mexico 87556
www.rennyrussell.com

Designed by Renny Russell
Edited by Linda Bevard
Printed by Midas Printing International Limited
Text: Bembo and Futura

Publisher's Cataloging-in-Publication
(Provided by Quality Books, Inc.)

    Cobb, John Candler, 1919–
    Fragments of peace in a world at war : photographs,
    poetry, and perspective / John Candler (Jock) Cobb.—1st ed.
        p. cm.
        Includes bibliographical references.
        LCCN 2010924237
        ISBN-13: 978-0-9760539-5-8 (hardcover)
        ISBN-10: 0-9760539-5-0 (hardcover)
        ISBN-13: 978-0-9760539-4-1 (softcover)
        ISBN-10: 0-9760539-4-2 (softcover)

    1. World War, 1939-1945 — Pictorial works.
    2. World War, 1939-1945 — Poetry.
    3. World War, 1939-1945 — Photography. I. Title.

    D743.2.C63 2011 940.53'022'2
        QBI10-600253

www.fragmentsofpeace.com

I would like to thank Renny Russell and the Animist Press team, who helped turn a pile of negatives and notes into the realization of a dream.

Matt Alexander of Picture Perfect, who lovingly scanned the 68-year-old negatives.

Charlie Edwards, friend and fellow ambulance driver, who contributed several of his poems for this work.

My children Nat, Julianne, Bethany, and Loren, and my wife Holly, without whose help and support this job might never have been finished.

Mankind must put an end to war, or war will put

an end to mankind. War will exist until that

distant day when the conscientious objector

enjoys the same reputation and prestige

that the warrior does today.

—John F. Kennedy

CONTENTS

Selemiye

Baalbeck

Alexandria

El Alamein

CAIRO ★

ranto

irte

PREFACE

Renny Russell

When my friend Nat Cobb asked if I would be interested in publishing a book of his father's World War II photographs, I was curious. But I was unprepared for the power of the images I saw when Jock Cobb and Nat arrived at my house with several boxes of framed silver gelatin prints and notebooks.

As I studied them and read the heartfelt haikus Jock had written to accompany the photographs, I knew his work must be shared, and I feel honored to be part of the historic publication of one of the most compelling collections of World War II photographs ever published.

On that hot July day in 2009, I began a journey with Jock by transcribing his faint pencil notes, then encouraging him to write the missing haikus and narrative, and working with him to obtain the highest-quality digital scans possible of his 35mm film negatives. Concluding each of the three sections of photos and poetry in this collection is his explanatory narrative elaborating on many of the images.

During this project, especially while he was studying the enlargements, Jock was flooded with emotions and memories that he had suppressed for decades to protect himself from the unimaginable horror and trauma that is war. By writing new narrative and poems, Jock has arrived at a peaceful plateau. Even though he received a medal for his service, he still cannot recall anything about the Battle of Monte Cassino in 1944, one of the most intense battles of the war. His photographs leading up to it document the coming madness and chaos that would leave more than 80,000 Allied soldiers dead.

In Part 1, Arab Friends and Teachings, Jock's photographs record an America at its best. Many are images of villagers and nomads who have come to medical clinics for smallpox vaccinations or treatment of severe diseases like malaria. During his time in Syria, Jock was assigned to the Hadfield Spears Mobile Clinic and drove Dr. Saleman, an Arab Jebel Druze physician, to the temporary clinics.

Other images capture sublime landscapes. In one we see Jock's ambulance dwarfed by the immense and wild roadless expanse of the Syrian-Iraqi Desert. His accompanying haiku reads:

not really lost in

magnificent desolation

driving by compass

Such photographs came alive when I learned that the ambulance once broke down when the drivers were a hundred miles out. Jock had to clean the points in his distributor with sandpaper he borrowed from a local Arab sheikh so they could drive back through the sand and mud before nightfall.

In Part 2, North Africa Desert War, we leave the relatively peaceful Middle East and view scenes that are hard to imagine in our age of so-called "smart" warfare. Through Jock's lens, we see images of drivers eating hardtack (dog biscuits), cooking canned corned beef (singe, as the French called it, or "monkey meat"), and stirring porridge over tin can stoves fired by sand soaked with gasoline. We see drivers bathing and boiling their dirty clothes in canisters, in country where gasoline was more plentiful than water.

boiling out the smell

of petrol, blood, sweat, and fear

essences of Hell

The haiku accompanying the image of a shirtless British doctor operating in 125° heat on a wounded German tank man reveals Jock's compassionate awareness that beneath the skin we're the same. It was a powerful moment and it was then he made the decision to go to medical school.

sweating with the knife

London surgeons doff their shirts

and save a German life

Some of those on the operating table were ambulance drivers who had struck land mines but hadn't fortified their floorboards with sandbags. Many didn't survive.

In Part 3, Italian Turmoil, we board an LST (landing ship for tanks) from North Africa and land in Taranto, Italy—and Jock's photographs increase in intensity. He captured horrific images. "Death at Tea" shows the bodies of British soldiers, who moments before had been drinking tea and reading mail from home, blown to pieces. This image prompted his most recent and poignant poem, "Anti-Personnel."

An image of a young boy perched on the back of a military truck and wearing a soldier's uniform has to be one of the most compelling antiwar photographs.

in dead soldier's uniform

he yearns for him he hardly knew

trying to understand

For relief, Jock found time to play chess with his comrades, tinker
with his ambulance, and read books like The Rubaiyat of Omar
Khayyam and War and Peace. At night he covered the windows
of his ambulance with blankets and plugged his photographic
enlarger into a dome-light socket. There, on a stretcher rigged
as his workbench, he developed film and made prints, watching
them materialize in the trays like a dream . . .

Jock captured the enduring human spirit in the face of unimaginable
terror—for example, a photo depicting a group of amused drivers,
scrounging much-needed parts from a trashed ambulance after its
accidental nighttime encounter with a Sherman tank. Jock recalls the
driver saying: "A tank rode over me and I was cold sober!"

Many of the images in *Fragments of Peace* have a humorous or
ironic twist—a pair of copulating camels (Jock titled the photo
"Camel Hump"); a donkey wandering among the ruins of a
bombed church in Fossacesia, Italy, on Christmas Day, looking
for something to eat; the civilian Dr. Cipolla dressed in neat suit
and tie, working his way through the high piles of rubble of
demolished buildings to make a house call.

During one conversation with Jock punctuated by long periods of
silence when words would have gotten in the way, I noticed on the
table next to him an enormous knife in a battered leather and wood
sheath. It was a *kukri* knife of the Gurkha—the legendary Nepalese
fighters of the old British colonial army who were used during
World War II as a suicidal frontal attack. The military didn't speak of
sending them in, rather of "turning them loose." The fighters never
removed the knife from its sheath unless to draw blood. A notch at
the end of the blade channeled blood away from the hand. This
knife had belonged to a Gurkha who died in Jock's ambulance.

Fate and circumstance spared Jock's life more than once. During
the battle of Enfidaville, a German 88mm bombshell landed
underneath his ambulance while he was carrying patients. It
failed to detonate. Another 88mm shell ripped through a fellow
driver's ambulance, destroying the instrument panel, shredding
the back of the driver's seat, flattening the tires, and missing the
gasoline tank by inches. It buried itself in the sand without
detonating. There's no doubt in Jock's mind that unknown
friends, perhaps German conscientious objectors enslaved in a
Nazi munitions factory, had tampered with the fuses!

Drivers endured the Nebelwerfer bombs, or "Moaning Minnies" —short-range rockets that were not particularly accurate but did have a crippling psychological effect. Many soldiers developed "battle fatigue" (today we call it post-traumatic stress disorder), in which a combatant so traumatized by war no longer cared to live and wandered aimlessly, often into enemy fire.

I was especially moved by Jock's special and enduring friendship with fellow ambulance driver Charlie Edwards, whose vivid and lyrical poems complement some of these photographs. This book is Jock's final offering to his old comrade before they, like so many other World War II veterans who have preceded them, fade into the twilight.

Fragments of Peace also pays homage to the men who risked their lives for their fallen comrades and to all the conscientious objectors during World War II who many Americans chastised and berated as cowards simply because they wanted to heal, not kill.

The constant of Jock's lifetime of service has been his work toward the betterment of mankind. He remains avidly against war.

As America wages endless war, Jock's 2009 poem "War Medals" —describing medals he received sixty years after the war had ended—resonates with its timeless antiwar message.

WAR MEDALS

Jock Cobb

Thoughts on receiving two shiny medals in the mail sixty years after World War II was over

War medals
would seem too gaudy on my chest.
I'd sooner wear
the blackened shards of jagged steel,
the flying shrapnel from the
 crashing bombs and shells,
that killed
too many drafted boys too young,
spilling out their warm red blood
so quick
we could not save them.

There was no way to mourn
so many wanton tragic deaths;
we hid
our tears, our horrors and our fears
and feigning calm,

we staunchly carried on.

Those horrors laced with fears,
long-festering deep inside the brain,
burst out at last, demanding,
"Wars must cease!"

We searched
this all-too-human world in vain
for any path to lasting peace.

Alas,
Those same ancestral fighting genes
That once helped Early Man prevail
now lead us down the nuclear path
to self-destruct
and fail.

INTRODUCTION

Me and my ambulance down in the mud

My service as an ambulance driver during World War II clarified in my mind what I wanted to do after the war. I had been greatly impressed by the wisdom and humanity of the officers and other ranks of the British Royal Army Medical Corps, especially the Kiwis (New Zealanders) and the Scotsmen of the Highland Division and the 51st Medium Artillery, with whom I worked in North Africa. They were trying to put back together what others were tearing apart. I decided I wanted to be a doctor.

I applied to the Medical School of the University of Otago at Dunedin, New Zealand. My Kiwi friends had highly recommended it, and I was interested in their new system of national medical care. I also applied to Harvard Medical School, where my father was a professor. But I didn't have much hope, and in the midst of war the thought of getting home and going to school seemed an impossible dream.

In the winter of 1944, after three days of rain, we were about to go in to support a tank assault in San Vito, Italy. I disliked "going in" to support the tanks in their noisy battles, even in good weather. Before breakfast, five of us volunteered to extricate our four-wheel-drive ambulances from the sticky mire. While we worked, a motorcycle messenger came skidding up from AFS Headquarters with a cablegram for me from my father—I had been admitted to Harvard Medical School starting in the summer. I crumpled it and put it in my battle dress pocket. It seemed a distant whisper from another world. I remember doubting I would even survive that day.

The day ended with Art Ecclestone and me aboard a British hospital ship not because of injury but because, with most others in our unit, we had succumbed to infectious hepatitis A, probably from drinking contaminated water. We steamed all night to Brindisi, on the heel of Italy, and in the morning were admitted to a recently fumigated Italian maternity hospital that the British had recently taken over. Our treatment—bed rest and a near-starvation diet supplemented by one quart daily of 20 percent glucose solution (yuck!)—was less than ideal and, being civilians, we signed out against medical advice. When I got into my battle dress, I was astounded to find the crumpled cablegram in my pocket and dumbfounded that I had done nothing about it. I answered it immediately.

My AFS friends and I had been living from hour to hour, suspending any serious thoughts about the future and doing what

crumpled cablegram

despite jaundice, mud and tanks

turned my life around

xvi

needed to be done in the front lines of that bloody war. Now, with a future to live for, my outlook changed. I was much less eager to volunteer for frontline action. I distanced myself from my friends who, by necessity, had put their future on ice, and took care to ensure that I would get home in one piece.

In the spring of 1944 I arrived in Milton, Massachusetts, and I spent the summer taking prerequisite biology courses. In my free time, long into the weekend nights, I printed 8-x-10-inch enlargements of my war photos in my tiny home darkroom, feeling compelled to share them with my family and friends. I entered medical school in September of 1944.

The excitement of studying medicine, and my anticipated future in public health, swept me up in a whirlwind that carried me through the arduous years of medical school, the stresses and joys of marriage and four children, and my busy internship and residency years. I spent four stimulating years conducting academic research at the Johns Hopkins School of Public Health and a fascinating four years as consultant in maternal and child health with the Indian Health Service in New Mexico. Next, our family spent four years in West Pakistan, where I was field director of the Medical Social Research Project on Population. I was working for and with the government of Pakistan, the Population Council, the University of the Punjab, Johns Hopkins School of Public Health, and the Ford Foundation.

When we returned to the United States, I was appointed professor and chairman of the Department of Preventive Medicine at the University of Colorado Medical School, where for twenty years I taught medical students and did more research. During sabbaticals and special leaves I had the good luck to work in ten third world countries consulting in maternal and child health and nutrition and family planning. These jobs were often with the World Health Organization, sometimes with the Quakers, and sometimes with other international organizations.

After my retirement in 1984, we moved back to our home near Albuquerque. Then, at last, I began to think back to World War II. I pulled out the enlargements, curled up in brown envelopes in a forgotten trunk, that I had printed forty years earlier. I mounted and framed some for exhibitions at the Albuquerque Museum, several AFS reunions, and a Unitarian Church and saw that many people were truly interested in the story they told.

As the United States continues to steer us into new and ill-advised wars, I feel an urgency to publish my photographs—along with poems and thoughts about World War II in particular and war in general—hoping to make a contribution toward peace.

My family and I hope that the poems and photographs may also strike a sympathetic chord with the many medics and wounded veterans and their families who must deal with the wounds of every war, including grief and the persistent mental problems of post–traumatic stress disorder and traumatic brain injury.

—Jock Cobb
Albuquerque, New Mexico
September 2010

NOTES ABOUT THE PHOTOGRAPHY

I had permission to use my cameras in action, being the official photographer for the platoon. I was able to avoid censorship by developing and printing the photos myself, in the ambulance when off duty at night.

I used two cameras: a 35mm Voigtländer folding camera with a 50mm Tessar lens, and a cheap and simple 35mm fixed-focus Argus automatic flash camera that had a wide-angle lens. I rarely used an exposure meter, trusting my experience and a good deal of luck, because the films, flashbulbs, and developers that I could buy or scrounge here and there were often strange to me.

In the back of the ambulance, using the ambulance battery, I made small prints with a Kodak portable enlarger. I mailed appropriate prints to the AFS in New York for use in recruiting and raising money.

Needless to say, there was a good deal of grief due to the primitive conditions, dubious water, widely varying temperatures, and ever-present chance that I might be suddenly interrupted by enemy shelling or called to ambulance duty.

In 1944 on my arrival in the U.S.A. by Liberty ship at Newport News, the customs officer impounded my negatives, but fortunately he mailed them on to me a few weeks later. I made enlargements in my tiny darkroom at home in Milton, Massachusetts, when I was studying biology in preparation for medical school.

My original negatives are stored in the archives of the University of Colorado in Boulder, Colorado, where they may be accessed by historians and other researchers for non-commercial purposes. The scanned photos used in this book, along with other material, may be viewed online at http://www.fragmentsofpeace.com.

OUR CROSSING:
NEW YORK TO EGYPT

In addition to our contingent of about fifty American Field Service volunteers, there were seven thousand American troops aboard the *Aquitania*. We crossed unescorted from New York City to Port Tewfik (Suez) in 1942.

We heard that all the troopships that had sailed from New York City bound for Egypt that summer had been torpedoed. We steamed at twenty-five knots, zigzagging all the way, watching for submarines and torpedoes.

The voyage, with stops in Rio de Janeiro and Cape Town, took forty days (September 21 to November 1). We arrived during the Battle of El Alamein. The rumor was "Port Tewfik is in flames." We didn't know whether we would even be able to go ashore.

Since I didn't have permission to use my camera on the troopship, I wrote the following sonnet trying to capture the image I saw as darkness fell the night before we docked.

TROOPSHIP AT DUSK

The moving sea tossed up a blue array
Of whitecapped shapes advancing toward the west
In vain, to keep the warm declining day
Whose rosy light enriched each wavelet's crest.
But even as they sped, ambitions high,
Tricolored peaks like flags for victory,
The graying night swept up the eastern sky
And dulled to fluid lead the colored sea.
The blackout bugle blasted through still air,
A soldier at the rail with chin in fists
Stood up, removed his helmet, smoothed his hair,
And left the darkened deck to night's cold mist.
That queen of seas, thus blended with the night,
Sped onward, hiding fears and hope and light.

ARAB FRIENDS AND TEACHINGS

Training
Egypt to Lebanon and Syria
November 1942–February 1943

distant guns rumbling

new recruits hiding fears of

rendezvous with death

it never rains

in the Western Desert,

or so we were told

after Alamein,

quiet breakfast, pondering

Pharaohs and fascism

Mena House Near Cairo, Egypt | Winter 1942–1943

ancient Baal temples

to gods of sun, wine, and love:

new young volunteers

busy wartime *souk:*

shoppers of differing faiths

seeking common fruit

Baalbek, Lebanon | Winter 1942–1943

at the old stone fort,

across language barrier,

she signals friendship

barefoot sister's love,

winter sun, and swaddling:

what prince had more?

Baalbek, Lebanon | Winter 1942–1943

wartime morning sun

melts ambulances' cloaks

of peaceful snow

weavers in the *souk*

have time to sit in the sun

and share their wise thoughts

Damascus, Syria | Winter 1942–1943

cone-shaped mud buildings,

storing farmer's grain, reflect

eroded mesas

early morning task:

mysterious and compelling

engine needs my care

Selemiye, Syria | Winter 1942–1943 | Photo by C. P. Edwards

motor wouldn't start

a hundred miles from nowhere;

friendly Arabs helped

communicating:

Jewish driver from New York

with friendly Arabs

spinning white wool yarn,

villager walks up the hill

to be with us

Arabs closely watch

smallpox vaccination

to see it's done right

Kafate, Syria | Winter 1942–1943

flies rest on cool wall

while Mukhtar and son take turns

smoking noisily

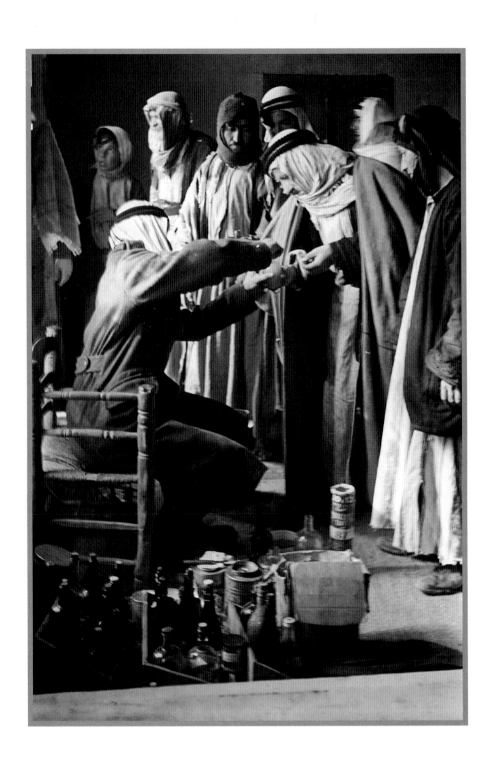

mobile pharmacy:

patients bring their own bottles

for medications

Kafate, Syria | Winter 1942–1943

shy village women

bake *khubus* in mud oven

ignoring camera

to please us, Mukhtar

puts on a show of camels

making boisterous love

ancient Roman fort

once drew water from this plain

now tilled by Arabs

not really lost in

magnificent desolation,

driving by compass

Syrian-Iraqi Desert | Winter 1942–1943

Bedouin mother

brings her twins in saddlebags

for vaccination

Jim prepares vaccine

for Bedouins migrating

across the desert

falcon on its perch

watches the vaccinations

of Arab children

servants of Emir

grind and brew bitter coffee

for Americans

guests and pet camels

are lodged and fed together

with tribal men

Emir's new Dodge

gift from general in Baghdad—

now "snafu"

Page 2

El Tahag Mobilization Camp, Egypt

Our first day at El Tahag Mobilization Camp, we worried about the ongoing Battle of El Alamein. John Barhydt is reading about it in *The Egyptian Mail*. Charlie Pierce (holding the magazine) later became an officer of our C Platoon. Dick Stockton, facing the camera with a worried look, was later killed in action. We didn't know then that this battle would be a victory for Montgomery's Eighth Army and a turning point for the Allies.

Page 3

El Tahag Mobilization Camp, Egypt

"It never rains in the desert"—this memorable quote came from Major Shaffer, who ordered us to spread our kits on the sand for inspection as dark clouds were threatening overhead. In memory of this baptism on our second day in Egypt, we

echoed his words at many a platoon celebration over the next sixty years.

Page 4

Mena House Near Cairo, Egypt

On leave, I had this view from my bedroom window, and a leisurely breakfast served at this terrace table. I wondered: What kind of power did those Pharaohs have? Were they universally revered as gods, or feared like fascist dictators? Far better to let the Jews go from Egypt, as the Pharaoh did in biblical times, than to persecute, incarcerate, and murder them as Hitler did!

Page 5

Baalbek, Lebanon

AFS headquarters was in Baalbek, Lebanon. AFS volunteer George Collins, later professor of art history at Columbia, filled us in on the history of the Baal religion and of these ruins dating from the first millennium B.C. To celebrate puberty, naked young men and women

worshipped at the temple of the sun god, got drunk at the temple of Bacchus, and wound up at the temple of Venus to make love. How different from the Puritan New England of my ancestors!

Page 6

Baalbek, Lebanon

Arab Bedouins, British soldiers, French engineers, Christian women, Jewish tradesmen, Danish missionaries, and many others all had business in the *souk* in Baalbek. Wearing their different headdresses, they lived and did business together in relative peace after the war shifted to North Africa.

Page 7

Baalbek, Lebanon

In those days, both Muslim and Christian women could be seen on the street without a veil. I'm told that the practice of women wearing the veil started in the early Christian culture of this region and was later taken up by the Muslims.

Page 8

Baalbek, Lebanon

Families were large. At that time, the population of Lebanon was about fifty-fifty Muslim and Christian, but the Muslims evidently had more children. This may have been a factor leading to the terrible communal strife that tore Beirut apart twenty-five years later.

Page 9

Baalbek, Lebanon

In Baalbek, we were billeted in unheated barracks previously occupied by the French Foreign Legion that were very cold in winter and barely sanitary. Also billeted there were Senegalese troops. In the afternoons they played soccer; the winners got the privilege of standing guard duty that night. They loved to carry a gun, even with only one bullet, and to challenge us as we came to the gate.

Page 10

Damascus, Syria

In this *souk* in Damascus, Syria, they sell, make, or fix

anything. It's a good place to sit and talk in almost any language. An Arab rug merchant explained to me in Spanish that a man who speaks just one language is only worth one man; a man who speaks two languages is worth ten men; and a man who speaks five languages is better than a whole army.

Page 11
Between Hama and Homs, Syria
These windowless adobe brick mud buildings between Hama and Homs, Syria, were used for human habitation and for storing farm produce. When the heavy rains came, they often collapsed. I've heard that building a very hot fire inside turns the clay to ceramic and makes them last better.

Page 12
Selemiye, Syria
We performed sixteen tasks, one a day, to keep our ambulances in good working order. Waiting for Dr. Saleman to finish his clinic in the tiny, remote village of Tel el Toot, I cleaned the distributor—I thought. But the engine wouldn't start, and we were 100 miles from a mechanic. Dr. Saleman correctly diagnosed that I had inadvertently got some dirt between the breaker points. He got some sandpaper from one of the older Arab men

(they used it to clean their guns) and cleaned the points. We got home before dark. I learned a couple of lessons!

I cleaned the distributor— I thought. But the engine wouldn't start, and we were 100 miles from a mechanic.

Page 13
Tel el Toot, Syria
While Dr. Saleman held his clinic, I walked up the *tel* (hill) to take this photo. It was then I foolishly undertook to do the daily task that involved cleaning the distributor.

Page 14
Tel el Toot, Syria
With a few words of Arabic and lots of gestures, we had surprisingly good conversations. Everyone had plenty of time to sit in the sun and really try to break through the language barrier. It was such a contrast to New York City, which we had left only two months before.

Page 15
Tel el Toot, Syria
This man joined the group communicating, mostly in sign language, with Jay

Nierenberg. Spinning while walking was an accepted activity for older men, who could do something useful—exercising and producing yarn—while remaining au courant in village affairs. It's better than in our culture, where retired old men too often just fall asleep in front of the TV.

Page 16
Kafate, Syria
Dennis Frome of the British Friends' Ambulance Unit was a trained vaccinator. But when he did it properly—that is, without causing bleeding—the Arabs objected. They would push their arms at him and insist, "Do more! Do deeper!" From sad experience, they knew the ravages of smallpox and the danger of not having a good vaccination.

Page 17
Kafate, Syria
Smoking the narghile (hubble-bubble pipe) was a social affair in the *menzoul* (guest reception room). The smokers handed the mouthpiece from man to man around in a circle. They usually mixed tobacco with hashish and sometimes with camel dung. Note the ever-present flies on the wall. After the clinic was over, Dr. Saleman would join us in the *menzoul*. Mukhtar (Mayor) Abou Brahim entertained us with stories and fables, and Dr. Saleman translated.

Page 18
Kafate, Syria
Bahjat, who was about my age, was our interpreter, medicine dispenser, orderly, and good friend. He called me Omar because he thought I looked like an Arab. He taught us to speak a little Arabic and to begin to understand Arab ways.

Page 19
Kafate, Syria
These ovens in Kafate were made of adobe mud, like the Pueblo Indian *horno* in the U.S. Southwest, but the only opening was at the top. After the fire was out, the women pressed the dough onto the walls of the oven to bake. The flat round loaves of *khubus* were thick, light, and tasty.

Page 20
Kafate, Syria
The village Mukhtar was suspected of hiding grain in ancient caves in the mountains, against British regulations, so he wanted to do something especially nice for the investigating British Army officer. He had his servants kill a lamb and prepare a splendid meal. He then invited us out to the courtyard to see a special show . . . The camels made such a trumpeting and squealing that the villagers, recognizing the sounds, came running. Perhaps the officer's heart was softened by this love scene.

Page 21
Near Selemiye, Syria
In the distance are the ruins of an ancient (probably Roman) fort built on a conical hill. We climbed up to it. Its very deep well probably collected water flowing from ancient tunnels under the surrounding plains.

Page 22
Syrian-Iraqi Desert
We had been driving for about 100 miles through the mud and into the Syrian-Iraqi Desert by compass. We climbed a hill to see if the Bedouin camp we were seeking was in sight yet. It wasn't—but I got this picture.

Page 23
Syrian-Iraqi Desert
On our way across the desert, we crossed paths with a tribe of Bedouins who came over to greet us. Bahjat, our interpreter, easily persuaded them all to be vaccinated, including the two small babies in the saddlebags on the donkey.

Page 24
Syrian-Iraqi Desert
Jim Hall of the British Friends' Ambulance Unit is getting the vaccine ready at the rear door of our ambulance. In the distance you can see some of the migrating tribe with their animals.

Page 25
Syrian-Iraqi Desert
I took this photo from inside the main goat-hair tent. The Emir had ordered the sidewall to be taken down so I could get this photo of the vaccinated children, our ambulance, the Emir's falcon perched nearby, and another tent in the distance.

Page 26
Syrian-Iraqui Desert
The *menzoul* was in the Emir's main tent, where he housed his six wives, eighteen children, and two pet racing camels. We slept in the honored place nearest the hearth, next to the camels. They draped beautiful carpets over saddles to make us comfortable. We sat around the fire and drank many small cups of bitter coffee. They ground the beans in the big wooden mortar and boiled them in elegant brass coffeepots settled among the embers. The servants filled the small brass communal cup for one of us at a time. Whenever that one handed it back, it was returned to him refilled. We learned to give the cup back with a twist of the hand to mean we had had enough.

Page 27
Syrian-Iraqi Desert
We dined royally on lamb and rice, which we ate

We rolled out our sleeping bags on the hearth near the dying embers. I didn't go to sleep until the camels dropped their heads and started to snore. I never learned who the mystery woman was, standing quietly in the dark while we ate.

carefully with the fingers of the right hand. A woman, probably one of the Emir's wives, stood quietly in the dark. I only noticed her years later as I studied the enlargement of this flash photo. We rolled out our sleeping bags on the hearth near the dying embers. I didn't go to sleep until the camels dropped their heads and started to snore. I never learned who the mystery woman was, standing quietly in the dark while we ate.

Page 28
Syrian-Iraqi Desert
At home, ordinary citizens could not buy a new car, and gasoline was severely rationed. Everything went to the "war effort." Great was my surprise when the Emir said, "I see you have a Dodge ambulance. Would you look at my Dodge? It is making strange jerking and banging noises." His friend the American general in Baghdad had given him the shiny new sedan the previous year. The gears were stripped, probably from improper clutch use and—ironically —from lack of lubricating oil. There were rumors that because of the enormous pipelines ESSO Standard Oil and other foreign oil companies were building, the Bedouins would no longer be able to move freely. The pipelines were too high for a camel to climb over and too low for it to crawl under. Oil companies were said to be reluctantly considering putting ramps over the pipelines at hundred-mile intervals. The goodwill Bedouins felt toward Americans was diminishing. This gave me an inkling of the insidious danger to the Bedouin way of life that was inherent in the development of Middle Eastern oil. A few years later I sold the few shares of ESSO stock my grandfather had given me. My banker thought I was crazy.

NORTH AFRICA DESERT WAR

Sand, Waste, and Victory
Egypt to Tunisia
March—October 1943

Cairo to Algiers

endless blowing sand, and years

of sweat, blood, and tears

Near Alexandria, Egypt | March 1943

tough British "tommy"

after years in the desert war

speaks quiet humor

from our bumf engine

heavy duty assignments

on flimsy paper

amid desert sands

forging strong from broken springs

desert smithy clangs

war had trashed their lands;

one of us who understands

trades and shakes their hands

Near Misurata, Tripolitania | March 1943

quietly alone

peace for body and for soul

before the raucous dawn

breakfast on the run

night breeze yields to scorching sun

convoy rumbles on

Tripolitanian Desert Near Sirte | March 1943

boiling out the smell

of petrol, blood, sweat, and fear

essences of Hell

no roadside café

war made hobos of us all

junkyard lunch today

Libyan Desert | March 1943

bloody red sunrise

foretold the Mareth battle's

cost in human lives

around the Mareth Line

Field Service ambulances

getting there on time

Wilder's Gap, Tunisia | March 1943

Britain's armored corps

spin and twist through Wilder's Gap

to end the desert war

tankman fried inside

hit by the Brits from the rear

wild sandstorm surprise

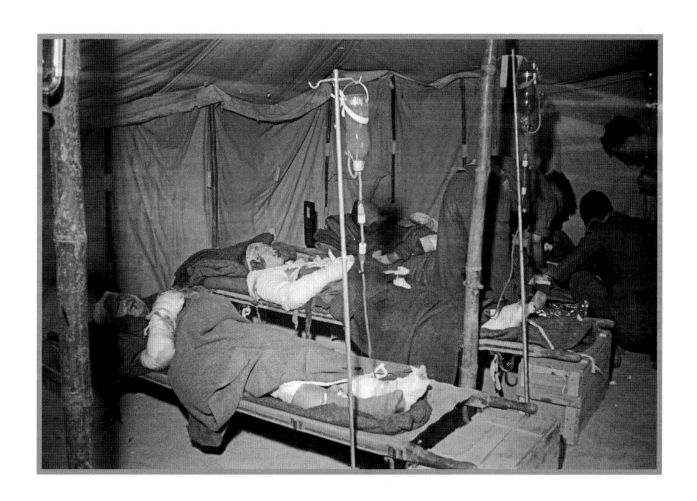

British medics help

Roman doc give Yankee blood

to German tank man

sweating with the knife

London surgeons doff their shirts

and save a German life

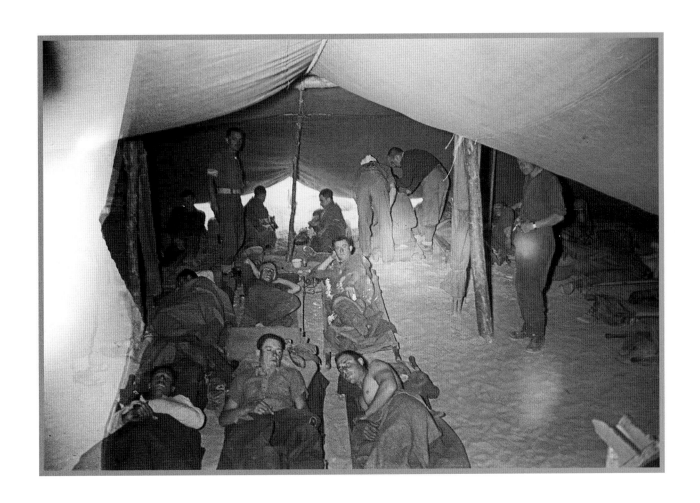

Italian doctor

treats willing German prisoners

in a British tent

one tough game of chess

warm sun and a book of verse

brought much-needed sleep

El Hamma to Gabes, Tunisia | April 1943

leaguered in a draw

near a barking ack–ack gun

wartime lullaby

THESE FOUR WALLS

Charles P. Edwards

Enfidaville, Tunisia, April 1943

By these four walls
carved in the hard clay
Where each breaking day
glistens
on the slant-wise strokes of the spade
I am held
not totally afraid
of the man-made thunder
and the singing of the steel.

Filled with wonder
I see
a fine filigree of pointed leaves
dancing above my eyes:
crown of wild olive and of pale
  green buds
wrapped in the silver sheen
of the whole tree.
I lie
beneath a three-branched trunk
lifting a canopy
of green
across the half-glimpsed sky.
This is my home, my castle,
cupped
in the embracing earth.

I die
a hundred deaths
while the serene air above my trench
is wrenched
by the musical march
of the shells, tunneling space:
a hundred singing voices in the clouds.

An invisible arch
of hot steel
flings across my back,
and dust
sinks softly about me.

I am clothed
in the palpitating earth,
my blood
keeps time to the resounding clay,
each thud
shatters the crystal day
into a thousand bits of humming steel:
cruel and jagged
spawn of a monster's womb.
Is my earth-shaped trench
a self-constructed tomb?

It has flown:
the spinning, high-toned, man-
  inspired dance.
I glance
about me, giddy and amazed,
cupped in the palm of the slow-
  turning world.
The sounds of birds in flight,
and the rich smell of the fast-
  ripening tree
cut in around me
like a surgeon's knife.

I am infinite,
immortal, filled with life,
more rich, more precious,
but more kin to death.

My life become more kin to death,
to men who do not walk in the
  parades,
draw breath,
or talk
the patient, laughing soldier words,
so other men can prate
about the dreams that soldiers die
  to make
and death their only fatherhood!

gunners could not know:

would their screeching lethal shells

land on friends or foe?

Italian soldier dead

Rome had pled neutrality

but nothing had been said

Takrouna, Tunisia | May 1943

in dugout command post

thoughtful gunner officers

contemplate reports

.

softly rolling waves

soothed our battle-jangled nerves

but the sadness stays

Near Enfidaville, Tunisia | May 1943

Abou Bakari

"Free French" soldier (or black slave)

thorny desert grave

by this peaceful shore

tangled wrecks of trucks and planes

scream the costs of war

By the Mediterranean, Tunisia | May 1943

cows graze peacefully

forgiving the violence

of yesterday

friend, who led us well,

leader of our C Platoon,

saved by a dudded shell

Volunteer Chan Keller

no more desert war,

those three thousand miles of sand

not worth dying for

officers and friends

raise their cups for peace at last

as war in desert ends

Near Enfidaville, Tunisia | May 1943

proud tank men astride

but I had seen too many

burnt alive inside

under cloudless sky

sparkling white-walled seaside town

which the war passed by

Monastir, Tunisia | May 1943

weavers in their shop,

idle looms and lots of yarn

wait for war to stop

heat and buzzing flies

olives ripen, grass turns brown

volunteers wait on

new engines at last

for tired ambulances

workshops working fast

scribes with ink and pen

sleep on sidewalk in the sun

waiting

dark sunken warship

becomes dock for loading blood

in Red Cross friendship

backing, hard to see

open jaws of landing ship

bound for Italy

Page 34

Near Alexandria, Egypt
While driving a recently repaired ambulance from Cairo to our assigned post with the British 12th Light Field Ambulance (LFA) at Marble Arch, the ambulance broke down again. We arranged for it to be fixed and hitched a ride with a friendly British officer in three-ton truck in a supply convoy. We lay comfortably on top of the cargo, which may have been explosives, and looked backward out through the open canvas truck cover, watching the desert unfold: from flat gravel with sparse grass, cactus, and desert shrubs, to rolling sand dunes with an occasional oasis. Sometimes we came close enough to see the waves of the Mediterranean and feel the cool, humid sea breeze, but most of the time it was just hot, dry, and dusty. I hated to see the desert strewn with an unbelievable array of war detritus: destroyed military

I hated to see the desert strewn with an unbelievable array of war detritus: destroyed military vehicles and war junk, evidence of two and a half years of prolonged, deadly, and violent fighting—a deadly soccer game.

vehicles and war junk, evidence of two and a half years of prolonged, deadly, and violent fighting—a deadly soccer game. The native people were wise to

stay out of sight and let our crazy war storm past.

Page 35

Libya
This British ambulance driver had been in the desert war three years when we arrived. He exemplified the toughness of the "tommies" and their quiet British humor. These large, heavy, two-wheel-drive Humber ambulances were standard in the British Eighth Army. They had trouble with loose sand or sticky mud, but did remarkably well. Our nimble four-wheel-drive Dodge ambulances were often assigned to frontline work. Notice the 12th LFA hospital tent in the background. In tents like this, not far from the front, they handled all kinds of wounds, did some surgery, gave plasma and blood transfusions, and stabilized the patients for transfer to base hospital—much like a MASH unit in the Korean War. Generally, we brought our stretcher cases from

the Regimental Aid Posts to the LFA.

Page 36

Tripolitanian Desert
This was the mobile field office of Captain Fred Hoeing of the AFS 11 Ambulance Car Company. Note the pair of AFS ambulances in the distance. The ambulances were dispersed in pairs at hundred-yard intervals to reduce risk in case of air attack. Fred, our genial volunteer "officer," can be seen under the tent stretched over his three-ton-truck "office" or "bumf engine," as we called it. (Bumf is short for bum fodder.) There he typed out our assignments on flimsy tissue paper.

Because we all had volunteered for the purpose of driving ambulances, we did not need a military hierarchal organization. The AFS was more horizontal—even "chaordic." Fred, himself a volunteer, was our liaison with the British officers. They requested, and he arranged for, the assignments of ambulances and drivers to the various military units in the field.

Page 37
Tripolitanian Desert
This blacksmith with the British Workshops Unit is repairing springs for our ambulances. He could fix or make most steel parts for them. The spring is laid out on the sand and the machine tools are inside the truck. The entire workshop could be packed up and moved inside of an hour. This unit was attached to us throughout the whole campaign and served us very well.

Page 38
Near Misurata, Tripolitania
We had plenty of tea in our British Army rations. This photo of Jay Nierenberg trading tea for eggs near Misurata shows how we paid for fresh eggs. The locals would appear in the desert, as if out of a mirage, holding up eggs. I never saw a living hen. They were wise to keep them with their women, safely hidden in an oasis like this one, or in their goat-hair Bedouin-style tents that blended into the desert landscape.

Page 39
Cyrenaica, Libya
In the wide-open desert, when our ambulances were dispersed as in this photo,

and the nurses were far away, we usually had no privacy. We would just dig a hole. One had to be quick to cover the shit with sand, because the scarab beetles, responding to the smell, came flying within minutes. They formed the shit into little balls about an inch in diameter and rolled the balls away to who knows where, to plant their eggs in. Having a high-class box like the one in this photo saved us the trouble with the shovel.

Page 40
Tripolitanian Desert Near Sirte
Chasing Rommel, we ate breakfast on the run (oatmeal, biscuits, jam, and tea) soon after sunrise. The ambulances were dispersed in pairs at hundred-yard intervals to reduce the risk of air attack, so it was a long walk to the cook truck. We ate sitting on the sand and then joined the convoy for another long day driving. At that stage in the war, the German planes usually tried to avoid hitting ambulances when strafing a convoy. That changed as things got worse for Rommel and the Germans.

Page 41
Cyrenaica, Libya
We had plenty of petrol (gasoline) brought by ship, but water was scarce. Here, Fox Edwards is boiling his clothes with a very small

amount of water and soap in a petrol tin. He is stirring them with a stick over a "desert stove"—a fire of petrol poured on the sand. Harry Hopper is hanging his clothes on a line between ambulances.

Page 42
Libyan Desert
We often were on an ambulance run, away from our mess, when mealtime came. Here, using the improvised desert stove and discarded German military junk for a table, Fox Edwards and Chan Keller are cooking.

Page 43
Tripolitania
In our pre-battle briefing, we learned that if the British Eighth Army did not break through the German-fortified Mareth Line, we would go with the 10th Armored Corps around it, driving south and west over Wilder's Gap in the sandhills. For this, each vehicle had been given rations of food— bully beef (corned beef), biscuits, and jam—and water (twenty ounces per man per day) enough to last nine days.

This route around the left end of the fortified Mareth Line had been discovered by a British "reccy" (reconnaissance) outfit that had sneaked through the desert in jeeps hundreds of miles

behind German lines many months earlier. The plan worked. The Germans were surprised from the rear and retreated in chaos. Many prisoners were taken, and we had many burned German tank men to transport. It was the beginning of the end for the German Afrika Korps.

Page 44
Wilder's Gap, Tunisia
It was a wild and noisy scene—hundreds of vehicles speeding, getting stuck, getting pulled out, churning and grinding on several parallel tracks through Wilder's Gap, around the left end of the Germans' fortified Mareth Line.

Page 45
Wilder's Gap, Tunisia
Fox Edwards and I were transporting a wounded German soldier with a broken leg. He was in great pain, so we had to go slowly. We fell behind our unit and were overtaken by the speeding, churning, and rumbling vehicles of the 10th Corps Armored Division. All medical units were on the move, so there was no place to leave him. His condition looked pretty bad. During a brief stop, I recognized our friends from a New Zealand hospital unit traveling on a track parallel to ours. I went over to get medical advice, but when I

got back our whole convoy had moved on, including Fox with our patient and, of course, all of my kit. The Kiwis took good care of me for a few days while all units were on the move. Finally, the 12th Light Field Ambulance (LFA), to which we were assigned, stopped near El Hamma and set up its hospital tents. There I found Fox, who had at last been able to deliver our patient for medical care. We worked night and day bringing in and caring for hundreds of seriously wounded and burned soldiers (mostly German tank men) who had been surprised by the attack.

British, German, and Italian soldiers all got the same treatment. Enemies of yesterday when wounded became brothers in pain and often helped each other while riding in our ambulance.

Page 46
El Hamma, Tunisia
German tank man being brought from the AFS ambulance into the 12th LFA Unit after the battle of Mareth—Rommel's Waterloo.

Page 47
Near El Hamma, Tunisia
The German Army Medical Corps had neither blood banks nor plasma in the field; they used live donors. Thus the German prisoners in our care were getting treatment they could not have gotten from their own medical corps. The Italian doctor in the background, also a prisoner of war, was helping the British orderlies to give American blood and/or plasma to these seriously burned men. British, German, and Italian soldiers all got the same treatment. Enemies of yesterday when wounded became brothers in pain and often helped each other while riding in our ambulance.

Page 48
Near El Hamma, Tunisia
In the intense heat of the midday African sun (around 125°F), this British Medical Corps surgical team had stripped to the waist. They left the tent wide open to catch whatever breath of wind there might be. They had been operating day and

---

They had been operating day and night, because there were so many seriously wounded patients, both British and German. The surgeon is searching for a bit of shrapnel in a soldier's groin.

---

night, because there were so many seriously wounded patients, both British and German. The surgeon is searching for a bit of shrapnel in a soldier's groin. I'm quite sure he was wearing sterile rubber gloves, even though they are not visible.

Page 49
El Hamma, Tunisia
Here German orderlies and an Italian doctor are helping the overworked British orderlies care for wounded German soldiers in a British LFA tent. (Italy was still fighting on the side of the Germans.) Earlier, during a rapid advance, we found the British 12th LFA had moved up even beyond

the ill-defined front lines and had been taken over by the German Medical Corps. The British and Italian doctors and staff were still there caring for the patients, both British and German. We left our patients there. The next day when we returned with more, the front line had moved up. We found it again under British command. The doctors and staff had remained with their patients.

Experiences like this convinced me that I, too, wanted to be a doctor. I saw that the medical professions were sanely trying to put people back together while everyone else in that crazy war-torn world had gone mad ripping everything apart. I applied to Harvard Medical School in the summer of 1943 and was lucky to be admitted when I got home nine months later.

Page 50
El Hamma to Gabes, Tunisia
This much-needed rest stop allowed us to forget the real war still raging, in its last throes before the surrender of Italian and German forces. Note my small traveling chess set on the ground. Taking turns at the wheel on such long drives, Fox Edwards and I would hand the folded-up chess set back and forth after making each move.

Fox, a poet himself, had been reading the book of verses in his hand when he fell asleep, perhaps dreaming of the Rubaiyat of Omar Khayyam.

Page 51
Tunisia

When traveling in convoy, we had to disperse our vehicles. This *wadi,* or draw, would give us some protection from possible shelling during the night, relieving us of the need to dig slit trenches. We were dog-tired after driving all day, so we rolled our sleeping bags out on the ground under the stars and had a good night's sleep.

Page 53
Enfidaville, Tunisia

Bob Orton and I were assigned to the Medical Aid Post of this British Eighth Army artillery unit during the last month of the battle for Tunisia. We got to know the officers pretty well—a jolly bunch when they weren't busy laying on a barrage. The big guns were aimed at Takrouna, where the Italian infantry soldiers were holding their last stand against an assault by the New Zealand Maori infantry. While the British Eighth Army was advancing toward Tunis from the east, the American army was advancing on Tunis from the west. We didn't know it at the time, but

Eisenhower was in England planning the D Day assault on the beaches of France; Rommel was back in Germany plotting an assassination attempt against Hitler; and Italy was soon to depose Mussolini and declare neutrality.

Page 54
Takrouna, Tunisia

After the surrender of Takrouna, Doc Brown, Bob Orton, and I, perhaps from morbid curiosity, climbed up to that stronghold. The 51st Medium Artillery had delivered a series of fierce barrages to "soften up" the Italians who were defending it. Shrapnel from one of "our" guns probably killed this Italian soldier; you can see the jagged holes ripped in his coat. It was disturbing for me to remember how close I had come to carrying the ammo to the guns that killed him.

With my field glasses I could see our position in the olive grove in the distance; I could see my slit trench where I had been lying when they were shelling us. I shuddered to remember how scared I had been, like the little bird that crapped on my head as enemy shells screeched through the trees and crashed around us.

After the fall of Tunis, Italy signed an armistice and became neutral.

Page 55
Enfidaville, Tunisia

In this dugout artillery command post, Major Leak is at the phone, Doc Brown is at his right, Dick Corse is standing. I got to know these officers well. They invited me to their mess even though I was only a volunteer civilian ambulance driver. We went through a lot together and became good friends, continuing to keep in touch long after the war.

One day while we were sitting at mess, the officer in charge of getting the shells up to the guns received an urgent order that a barrage on Takrouna must start in five minutes. I knew how shorthanded he was, because I had carried out several of his men who had been wounded. I had been on the point of offering to help him, but I suddenly realized that if I did, I would be involved in killing people, to which I was conscientiously opposed. I sat on my hands.

Page 56
Near Enfidaville, Tunisia

Doc Brown and Bill Cobb, both officers of the 51st Medium Artillery, with Bob Orton and me, both AFS ambulance drivers, got away from the

war for a few hours. In the foreground, you can see my blanket and book, Tolstoy's *War and Peace.* We were soothed by the wind and the waves, but the myriad heart-rending tragedies of war hung on.

Page 57
Somewhere in the Tunisian Desert

Abou Bakari, whose name is on the cross on the left, was probably a black African Muslim soldier/slave with the "Free" French forces of the British Eighth Army. Lacking stones, they covered these graves with prickly pear (*Opuntia*) cactus pads for protection against wild animals.

I served briefly as a relief ambulance driver with the Free French but have forgotten or blocked out most of that experience. I don't even remember taking this picture, but I can remember the inhuman way they treated their black African soldier/slaves.

Page 58
By the Mediterranean, Tunisia

There were hundreds, perhaps thousands, of military junkyards scattered all along the North African coast after the years of back-and-forth fighting in the North African campaign of World War II.

Page 59
Tunisia

But for the luck of the draw, either Chan Keller's ambulance or mine could have looked like this one, blown to smithereens. Coming upon this ambulance a month after the North African war was over made me remember with a shudder the rough times just weeks earlier, in April 1943, when we had luckily escaped such a fate. While returning to my post with the 51st Medium Artillery near Enfidaville after a hospital run, I had come suddenly into the open and under enemy fire. A German 88mm shell landed under my ambulance and buried itself in the sand without detonating.

The 88mm shells were the ultimate in German technology, yet many of the shells fired at us that month were duds. We think someone in Germany's munitions factories had been fixing the fuses so that they failed to detonate. I like to think we owe our lives to friends we never knew, perhaps German conscientious objectors to war who were forced to work in these factories.

Page 60
Volunteer Chan Keller

In April 1943 near Enfidaville, Chan Keller was standing on the

The 88mm shell struck his ambulance below the left windshield cowling, making an 88mm-diameter round hole through the instrument panel and the back of the (unoccupied) driver's seat. It destroyed the spare and rear tires, barely missed the gas tank, and buried itself in the ground without exploding.

bumper of his ambulance, looking through his field glasses to see where the shelling was coming from. To the German artillery marksman he must have looked like an enemy artillery officer on his staff car. It was a pretty good shot at nearly point-blank range. The 88mm shell struck his ambulance below the left windshield cowling, making an 88mm-diameter round hole through the instrument panel and the back of the (unoccupied) driver's seat. It destroyed the spare and rear tires, barely missed the gas tank, and buried itself in the ground without exploding. Understandably, Chan was shaken to the core. He was still a bit "bomb happy," laughing inordinately and shuddering, as he told me about it later.

In North Africa, the Germans generally respected the red crosses that were clearly marked on all our ambulances. As things got worse for the German army in Italy, we had to camouflage the ambulances at forward posts, because the red cross seemed often to be a target.

Page 61
Tunisia

In this recently set up prison camp, just after the fall of Tunis, the German officers looked grim, but the young soldiers looked numbed and confused. They had not yet been informed that Algiers had also fallen to the American army and that the whole African campaign was over. When we told them, at first they hardly believed it, but then they seemed to be relieved that the war was really over for them.

This photo shows little organization, no armed guards, and no high fences. If the prisoners had wanted to escape, where, in fact, could they have gone?

Page 62
Near Enfidaville, Tunisia

Celebrating victory by drinking whiskey with us were most of the junior officers of the 51st Medium Artillery, our special friends (clockwise from left): officers Bill Cobb and Gordon Ellis, bombardier Jones (medical orderly), Bob Orton (AFS volunteer), and officers Dick Corse, Doc Brown, and Tom Jones.

At midnight, the colonel, whom we had neglected to invite, torpedoed our party, said we were too rowdy, and sent us all to bed. We felt like a bunch of bad boys who had been caught at some mischief in boarding school. We went sheepishly to bed.

Page 63
Tunisia

During the Battle of Mareth we had seen so many severely burned tank men. When a tank is hit by an armor-piercing shell, the men inside are incinerated.

Page 64

Monastir, Tunisia

After the Tunisian campaign and German Afrika Korps surrender, my ambulance had a broken spring. Since our workshops were on the move, there was no place to get it fixed. I couldn't keep up with the convoy. I had to drive it very slowly back from Tunis, along the coast to our leaguer near Tripoli.

Being alone, I stopped to swim and visit in little towns along the way, including the old walled town of Monastir. I met so many wonderful, welcoming French-speaking Tunisians. It was a very rewarding experience and a relaxing journey.

Page 65

Monastir, Tunisia

Monastir had been a welcome rest stop on my drive back to Tunis. Thirty-five years later, while I was back in Africa to consult with Project Hope on a new public health program, my wife and I were able to enjoy this lovely historic town under better circumstances. We lived in a rented house for a couple of months and traveled out to the rural areas, where we were setting up public health clinics. We bought some of the beautiful blankets woven by the local people and visited places I had seen during the war,

including oases and underground villages whose houses were nearly buried beneath the sand, where it was twenty degrees cooler. And, of course, we visited the museum in Carthage.

Page 66

Tripoli, Libya

We had been waiting six months under these olive trees for our chance to go with the British Eighth Army to Italy. Here our group, mostly C Platoon, is gathered at midday in the shade of the olive trees, where the temperature was about 120°F. We would gather like this at siesta time to listen to records, write letters, read, play games, or just sit and think.

We all did more substantial things, too. I took a British Army course on disarming enemy mines and shared the knowledge with my platoon. I also spent a few weeks learning auto mechanics in our workshops and helped put a new engine in my ambulance.

In the middle of the group, with the sun on his hair, is Vern Preble, who was killed when he drove over a tank mine in the Battle of the Sangro River soon after we got to Italy. To Vern's left are Joe Wolhandler and Luke Kinsolving (reading). In the foreground (swishing a

fly) is John Leinbach. To John's left is Chan Keller, sitting on a stretcher playing checkers with Ralph Beck. Beyond Chan, with their backs to the ambulance, are Fox Edwards and Jay Nierenberg sitting on the stretcher, reading. We were bonded together by our shared war experiences and continued to keep in touch through reunions for more than sixty years.

Page 67

Near Tripoli, Libya

Sergeant Jack Oxley ran the British Army Workshops in a genial and effective way, as I found out when I volunteered to help put a new engine in my ambulance. It was a job getting the ambulances ready for the Italian campaign after the new engines finally arrived from the USA.

I helped fitter Jack Skinner, who is shown on the left in this photo. In the shade of the olive trees, from sunrise to sunset with a siesta in the hottest part of the day, we worked for a few weeks on these poor old tired ambulances. I learned a lot and enjoyed having something important to do after that long hot summer of waiting.

Page 68

Kairouan, Tunisia

While waiting for the new engines to be installed, a

few of us spent a day driving to Kairouan, one of the great holy cities of Islam. We visited the mosque and toured the city. These scribes, waiting to write a letter for anyone, touched a sympathetic chord.

Page 69

Tripoli Harbor, Libya

This hospital ship was probably on her way to Italy. The dock is a ramp constructed on top of a sunken warship that was lying on its side in the mud of Tripoli Harbor. The blood we were loading had been donated by volunteers like us while we awaited our U.S. Navy landing ships, tanks (LSTs) to drop us on the Italian Navy docks in Taranto, Italy. We knew Italy had withdrawn from the war and declared neutrality and that the German army had fiercely fought against the invasion of Sicily, but we didn't know how we would be received in Taranto. As it turned out, we were well received by the Italian Navy and all the Italians we met on shore. Sixty years later the AFS was invited by the City of Taranto and the Italian Navy to celebrate the sixtieth anniversary of that day.

Page 70

Tripoli Harbor, Libya

Backing into the bow of an LST bound for Italy.

ITALIAN TURMOIL

**Tragedy and Strength
Italy
November 1943–April 1944**

aboard LST

warm sun, music, and smooth sea

calmed our doubt and fears

crumpled cablegram

despite jaundice mud and tanks

turned my life around

waves on rocky shore,

mines guard old stone harbor fort

fishing boats pulled out

by one candlelight

reading Tolstoy's *War and Peace*

and writing letters home

BATTLEFIELD CROSS

Charles P. Edwards

Where armies sweep across the ravaged plains,
burdened with ruins of historic years,
thrust at a grave bereft of burial tears—
cold barren earth to harbor youth's remains—
there springs a wooden cross darkened by rains
which course the furrowed cheeks of human fears
and pound upon the earth-encrusted ears
of mute, unknowing and unwept-for names.

Beside the shattered tank the wood cross stands
and wears a tattered garland at its feet.
it leans, outstretched, against the smoking land
where thundering earth and flaming sky still meet.
It leans, unsteady, for two bone-ribbed hands
lift but a symbol of mankind's defeat.

a fierce tank battle

ripped away the quietness

and cut short a life

posing for this photo

just out of the hospital

we tried to look tough

we loved his tousled

boyishness; Preb made us laugh

when laughing was hard

It took guts to say

"guess I won't drink any beer

for awhile. . ."

Near Lanciano, Italy | December 1943

PREB

Charles P. Edwards

Written in memory of Vernon Preble, mine casualty, Sangro River battle, Italy, November 28, 1943

They wrapped him in an American flag
and stuck a wooden cross in the soft ground
  at his head.
It was his last slit trench.
"I guess I won't drink any beer for a while"
was all he said
when they pulled his burned body free.

The fire
had scorched his eyes
his face
his hands and body.
Pinned down
in the torn and mangled ambulance,
trapped,
he fought clear of the flames
in the sickening seconds after the roar
of the bursting mine.

It was a brave fight
for life.
He lived four days more.

They found him
beside his ambulance
that the mine had burned and killed.

An ambulance in war
is part of those who live in it,
drive it over steep hills and through rivers
where shells are dropping.
It is like a live thing
helping wounded men,
and where men who cannot be saved
sometimes die.
His ambulance would not go on without him.

They picked him up
from beside the charred wheel
that he had held
at Mareth,
Enfidaville,
the Sangro River.
His life meant many lives saved.

We loved him
for his tousled boyishness,
and because of the times
he made us laugh
when laughing was hard.
It took guts
to say
"Guess I won't drink any more beer. . ."

these frontline soldiers

deeply sympathized with my

objection to war

wars worst terrors dwell

in mind's darkest prison cell;

break-out raises hell!

ANTI-PERSONNEL

Jock Cobb

Albuquerque, New Mexico, January 2010

That bomb from hell (called "anti-personnel")
  probably exploding in their midst
had scattered wide their body parts and kits,
so I couldn't count how many men
it killed—surely more than ten.
Driving by, I'd seen that I must try
to photograph Grim Reaper's grisly job
for all the world to see, to glean—and sob.

These battle-weary tommies at the front,
fighting for a mountain pass to Rome,
were stopping for a needed break, at last,
brewing tea and reading mail from home,
when HELL broke loose! A BLINDING
  FLASH AND BLAST—
Unread letters ripped from love-clenched fists
were strewn among their bodies blown to bits.

One man alone, by luck, escaped the blast.
With shoulders stooped and trembling
  body bent,
he blindly stared as if his mind were rent,
his addled brain in utter disbelief.
A living statue of both guilt and grief,
he may have thought it was his fault

to choose that time to take a walk.
—had he but known.
I was not kind
to him, who had no wounds to show,
—only in his mind.
I'd learned to care for wounds of
  flesh and bone.
What could I do for him: so sad, so mad,
—and so alone?
"ANY RANDOM ACT OF HUMAN
  KINDNESS,"
—had I but known. . .

Instead, with trembling hands and
  quaking tread,
I tried to go and photograph the dead;
Shaken up by all that had occurred,
my camera shook, my photographs were
  blurred.

Sad and overwrought, I hurried then
to my waiting ambulance and men
whose body wounds I understood, I thought
—HAD I BUT KNOWN.

90

utter disbelief

a living statue of

both guilt and grief

scattered body parts

of soldiers drinking tea and

reading mail from home

Near Mozzagrogna, Italy | December 1943

well-aimed German guns

enforce the NO PARKING sign

in HELL FIRE LANE

barefoot refugees

walk home across the Sangro's

military bridge

Near Sangro River, Italy | December 1943

a narrow escape;

when it shakes you to the core,

it's hard to laugh away

NO PLACE FOR KIDS

Charles P. Edwards

To Denny Hunt, wounded in action, Italian campaign, January 1944

> *Please, dear God, do this job yourself and don't send your son,*
> *Jesus Christ, because it is no place for kids.*
>
>   —*Cowboy prayer*

It was no place for kids
so the old cowboy went himself
sitting straight
as if it were a horse he was riding
instead of the cramped front seat
of an ambulance.

His horse
would have brought him safe,
but the old cowboy
missed the turn
where the sign said "Mines". . .
someone had moved the barrier.

The front wheel
crunched
on the plate-like top
of the tank mine.

There was not much left of his ambulance.
The engine was blown clean out,
and the two seats
blown through the doors,
and the old cowboy
inside

with one leg like pulp
as high as a cowboy boot could reach.

"Here's your fountain pen,"
he said
to his fellows at the R.A.P.
"I've brought you your fountain pen,"
as they inched him
agonized
out of the tin-can ambulance
that had no brains
like a cowboy pony.

Something that a soldier means by "chance"
when a fellow gets his leg blown off
his last trip up.
But the old cowboy
was going to ride again.
You have to let God handle things
in war.

It must have been God
and not God's son
that saved him –
because it was no place for kids.

a real cowboy

who hit a mine and lost a leg

back in the saddle

welcome rest at last

parked on Marchese's terrace

above peaceful farms

Pollutri, Italy | December 1943

Marchese's nieces

teaching us Italian

soothing war-stressed nerves

C Platoon and friends

attempting to be merry

singing bawdy songs

mourning war–lost sons

she sits on stone steps, spinning

as the sun goes down

we, so far from home,

needed them, and they us,

to dispel war's gloom

too soon we had to

leave our peaceful Shangri–la

and return to war

in dead soldier's uniform

he yearns for him he hardly knew,

trying to understand

San Vito, Italy | December 1943

she took heart to find

in the ruins of her home

one ancestral rug

train tracks hang useless

over ruined Ortona

and calm boatless sea

Near Ortona, Italy | January 1944

demolition

returned humans to caves, and

was hell for donkeys

town and church half gone

dazed survivors struggle on

destitute but strong

Ortona, Italy | January 1944

Kiwis asked for us

for their Cassino assault

we'd been desert chums

engine maintenance

to keep it in top shape for

Monte Cassino

sans spit–and–polish

our seasoned ambulances

rejoined the Kiwis

tents in rain and mud

were homes for Kiwi medics

those damp winter months

Presenzano, Italy | January 1944

working for our supper

we pushed out our supply truck

up to hubs in mud

CASSINO

Charles P. Edwards

A sign
points "Hotel des Roses"
among burnt mounds of stone.
Green slime
creeps along interlocking craters.
A splash of flowers
fades
on a grave beside an unearthed mine.
Charred trees lean, alone.

The bare flank of "hangman's hill"
looks out with death's eyes
marked
in steel rims lashed
along each still
and naked street.
Stone blocks
teetering end on end
on amputated feet
push rubbled sand
onto the one road through.
Stores, school, homes
turned back to dust;
and in the turning
men
had lived and crawled and fought
and died
in cellared catacombs.

Cassino was thrust
into the mountain side,
stepped on by tanks,
crushed

under the weight of bombs,
mauled in the mad tide
of the march of war:
mortar and flame and rocket,
"creeping" and "box" barrage,
bayonet charge;
the Ghurkas at night with
    knives swinging,
bomb-crazed Jerries captured, singing
beside the shattered Abbey;
"A.P." "H.E." "Pin-Point" and
    "Saturation"
spelling annihilation;
a steel hat spinning in a rain-soaked trench
blown in the blast of a thrown grenade
or picked off by the sniper's telescopic
    sight;
infantry patrol at night
threading the fields sown with mines;
the roar of flight on flight
drowned in the puffed clouds
of air descended death.

Cassino
is one more name
etched into world-embittered fame:
wrought
to the proud, fanatic German will,
bought
by the nations charged to die or win
whose sons returned again, again
to kill
to storm and take the monastery hill.

brewing up some tea

a quiet time for thinking

before the assault

between rain showers

we could sometimes sneak a meal

without getting soaked

Near Monte Cassino, Italy | January 1944

rumbling up at night

with no lights, a Sherman tank

bumbled over him

TO MOTHER

Charles P. Edwards

If it must be that I am meant to die—
unknown, unhallowed in a foreign land
where Death, so cold, had led me by the hand
far from the bleeding earth and the torn sky:
in your heart, Mother, my love will cry
carried across the sea and shifting sand
by winds that reach beyond the crimson land
where streaks of heaven-sent clouds pass by.

The western wind will envy my soul's flight
even in death. Perhaps, the sky will weep
for me; and mountains, though I die unsung,
will clothe themselves in splendor in the night.
I will not heed these things, but I will keep
the love you gave to me when I was young.

graves and blown-up tank

adorn our brick house aid post

out in no-man's-land

atop her castle

first bloom of War's dark winter

aloof, she charmed us all

Casoli, Italy | March 1944

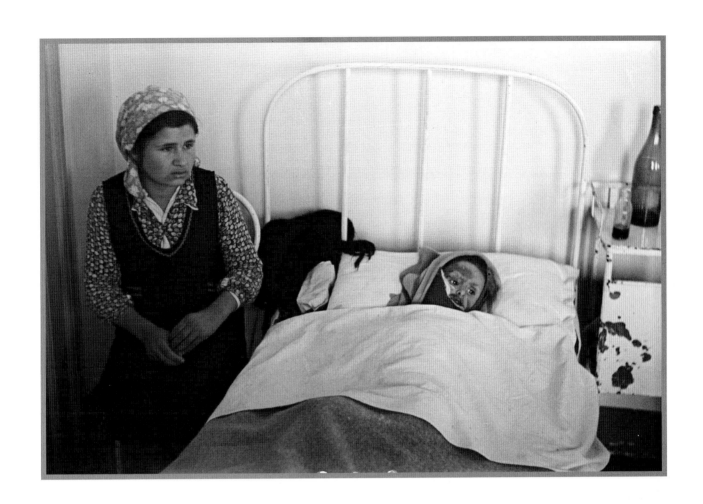

I found out first hand

that civilian hospitals

needed everything

soldiers and villagers

worked close together on

this conical craggy hill

Near Casoli, Italy | March 1944

army's glass ceiling

kept Indian officers

from having command

Civitella, Italy | March 1944

older women chat

casually ignoring

soldiers and armor

Civitella, Italy | March 1944

Doctor Cipolla

visits patients in the ruins

wearing neat black suit

in civilian clothes

Coco, chief guerilla, checks

scrounged machine gun

Civitella, Italy | March 1944

lucky to survive

carried to my ambulance

by luckier friends

hawser holds me up

both ships rocking crazily

over rolling seas

Page 78

Approaching Italy

Sailing across the Mediterranean in convoy, it took us several days aboard this American LST to reach the naval port of Taranto on the instep of the boot of Italy. We slept in our ambulances and ate good old U.S. Navy food. It was a smooth and comparatively luxurious crossing.

Page 79

Italy

Me at the rear door of my ambulance in sunny Italy.

Page 80

Termoli, Italy

We were billeted in Termoli for a few weeks. Several of us came down with jaundice (infectious hepatitis), probably from the polluted water. We were too sick to work but not sick enough, we thought, to be evacuated. So we took sick leave in a nearby recently abandoned, once splendid home of a prominent

Fascist. Having no firewood, we burned the Fascist literature, and eventually also the shutters and some of the furniture.

After a week of this luxury, a British colonel officially commandeered the house and we had to go. We were afraid we might be evacuated by ambulance down the line to a makeshift military hospital.

Page 81

Termoli, Italy

We moved into a building that had been used by the German army, but we had no material to black out the windows, and had to keep our use of light to a minimum.

Page 83

Between San Giacomo and Termoli, Italy

Here, the northerly-advancing British fought off a fierce German counterattack. The Adriatic Sea lies peacefully on the horizon.

Page 84

Bari, Italy

Art Ecclestone and I talked our way aboard a hospital ship in the Termoli harbor, hoping it might take us to England. Soon after we were under way, a German plane dropped a bomb that barely missed the ship. The ship unloaded us at the port of Brindisi, where they put us in a former maternity hospital that had just been fumigated and taken over by the British.

They only had field rations for food. We were not allowed to eat bully beef because of our hepatitis, and we were losing weight on only tea and biscuits, so they gave us 20 percent glucose solution to drink. Yuck! Being civilians, we could sign out against advice. We were very weak, but managed to hitch a ride to Bari. There we found a nice room in the home of an Italian woman who cooked for us, even a turkey dinner for Thanksgiving! Revived, we

returned to our platoon. They were all very busy at the battle for the Sangro River crossing, where Vern Preble had just been blown to smithereens by a mine.

Page 85

Ambulance Driver Vern Preble (Preb).

Page 86

Near Lanciano, Italy

Preb's grave near the Sangro River.

Page 88

Sangro River, Italy

Here on the north bank of the Sangro River, a Bren Gun Carrier brought stretcher cases from places that even my four-wheel-drive ambulance (far left) could not reach. The medic is holding up a plasma transfusion bottle for the patient lying on top of the carrier.

The closer I got to the frontline soldiers in action, the more appreciation I found for my conscientious objection to war.

Page 89

Sangro River, Italy

I was on the way to my post at the frontline dressing station when mortar bombs began to fall on the road ahead and behind, setting fire to several trucks. I was sure my ambulance would be hit next. Scared to dumbness, I jumped out and ran into this field and lay down in the shallow ditch in the foreground. I took my helmet off my head and placed it over my privates. (In bull sessions we had agreed that without those, life would not be worth living.)

An airborne bomb came toward me and exploded just beyond me, and I blacked out. Coming to, I shook myself and realized I was not hit. I lay there shivering for quite a while. I could see that my ambulance was OK.

Suddenly I realized how stupid I had been to run into this field—it had probably not been cleared of mines! When the shelling finally stopped, I stood up, shaking, and took this photo. Then I retraced my footsteps—very carefully—and drove off.

But for this photo, the whole terrifying experience would probably have remained blocked from my conscious mind, as were almost all the details of the Battle of the Sangro—except those memories that sixty years later come slowly sneaking back. Studying this photo now, I feel acutely uncomfortable and begin to taste the fear again. I still have no memory of the rest of that day. Were there any victims burned in those trucks? Did I take them back to hospital, or continue to my post? If there were no victims or survivors, I probably went on in a daze. My memory is still blank for most of the rest of that period we were working in the region just north of the Sangro.

Pages 90, 91, 92

Near Mozzagrogna, Italy
North of the Sangro River

There were about a dozen of them—they were hard to count; body parts were scattered all around. I was so upset that I forgot to focus my camera and had trouble holding it steady.

---

near Mozzagrogna, these tommies had been sitting in a circle drinking tea and reading mail from home. They probably took a direct hit from a mortar bomb or anti-personnel mine. There were about a dozen of them—they were hard to count; body parts were scattered all around. I was so upset that I forgot to focus my camera and had trouble holding it steady. Many decades later as I perused my rejected prints, the guilt and woe I had buried welled up and set my heart a-quake.

Page 93

San Vito, Italy

The sign was appropriate; this square in front of the Medical Dressing Station in San Vito remained under spasmodic German shelling for months. While I was fortunately inside the dressing station, my ambulance, seen here at the right, picked up a few more shrapnel holes. One piece of shrapnel penetrated one of my books. The truck at the left had taken a direct hit and burned.

Page 94

Near Sangro River, Italy

After the Battle of the Sangro, refugees could walk across the temporary Engineering Corps bridge that replaced the old stone bridge demolished by the Germans. They seemed so happy to be going home at last that when I asked

them to pose, they smiled as if the whole thing was just a jolly picnic at the beach; so I photographed them from behind.

Page 95

Pollutri, Italy

One night in December, while Tom Hale was driving wounded patients near San Vito, a shell exploded nearby. Shrapnel crashed through the window, tore his sleeve, and shredded his instrument panel. After a month of R&R at Pollutri, he was able to laugh about it—and shudder.

Page 97

Volunteer Denny Hunt

Denny Hunt, who lost a leg when his ambulance hit a mine.

Page 98

Pollutri, Italy

Exhausted and somewhat bomb-happy, we were pulled back a few miles from the Battle of the Sangro for much-needed rest and rehabilitation. We were billeted in the Marchese's stone residence in this ancient fortified town of Pollutri on a steep crag. It was our Shangri-la. The Germany army had conscripted the young men for labor and left the town intact. From the brick terrace we had this glorious view of the valley below.

I slept on a stretcher in the back of my ambulance, preferring this to the cold, cavernous sleeping quarters in the palace, where we had our mess. With the engine idling, I used the heater for warmth and the dome light for reading in bed. The Marchese would visit in the evenings and we would play chess. My Italian was very poor, and he was not very good at English, but the chessboard was a bridge that helped us communicate quietly.

Page 99
Pollutri, Italy
The Gerbasio family, refugees from Naples, were the nieces and nephew of the Marchese (facing the camera looking at photographs). They all were very hospitable, and we learned a lot of Italian in a most pleasant way. Note the glasses of wine and the happy smiles.

Page 100
Pollutri, Italy
On Christmas Eve, the platoon had a big party at our illustrious billet (the electric lights had come on; what luxury!). "Lofty," one of our British cooks, did nobly on the accordion. A couple of local Italian boys somehow got into the party, too.

Page 101
Pollutri, Italy
Grieving the loss of her own sons, Francesca Mauro would sit in the sun on her doorstep, spinning quietly. She loved to cook for us.

With the engine idling, I used the heater for warmth and the dome light for reading in bed. The Marchese would visit in the evenings and we would play chess.

Page 102
Pollutri, Italy
Having lost their two sons during the war, Maestro Mauro and Francesca needed us; and we, so far from home, needed them. We would bring them a can of bully beef, and they would cook *spaghetti a la guittara* for us in a big iron pot hanging over their hearth fire. We became their family.

Page 103
Pollutri, Italy
The girl on the left was an adopted refugee from a demolished town nearby. Pollutri had miraculously been spared from the ravages of the retreating German army. Now we had to leave this oasis and return to war-torn reality.

Page 104
San Vito, Italy
This fatherless boy, like so many in the war, was searching for something he did not understand and could not find.

Page 105
Ortona, Italy
Ortona was the eastern anchor at the Adriatic Coast of the German Winter Line or Gustav Line that bisected Italy south of Rome. Along this line from November 1943 through May 1944 some of the most difficult and bloody battles of World War II took place. Cassino is well known, where three offensives destroyed the city and the abbey above it.

Ortona, although not as well known, was equally bloody, with door-to-door fighting even on Christmas Day 1943. It was liberated by the First Canadian Division of the British Eighth Army. There were Canadian, as well as German and Italian civilian, dead—more than a thousand each, respectively—and despite a heroic effort, the city was destroyed. The liberation of Rome had been the objective; the Gustav Line was eventually broken at Cassino in May 1944, and Rome was liberated June 4. (We of AFS were posted with the Eighth Army, including the Canadians.)

The last stanza of Charles P. Edwards's poem "On the Beach—Ortona" says:

Until the old world
and the new
together seek and reach
the way
to Peace on Earth,
the winds of war
too soon
will build and blow
your lovely beach
away.

Much more than the lovely beach is at stake: the wisdom, the social mores, and the constraints on antisocial behavior that have been built up over the ages may all be lost as a tragic result of total war. I am sure that CPE would agree with me.

Page 106
Near Ortona, Italy
In October 1943, when we were billeted in the former home of an escaped Fascist official in Termoli, I found an old Fascist magazine proudly showing pictures of this Adriatic Coastal Railroad when it was new. It was touted as one of the great achievements of the Fascist regime. It had been Mussolini's pride!

Top-notch engineers had evidently designed this railroad and probably also the gigantic diabolical machine to destroy the same railroads. It was hooked onto the rear of the train and demolished the railroad as it retreated slowly up the track. A huge swinging hammer would knock out short pieces of track at regular intervals. This was, I guess, a product of the famous German expert engineering that also had produced the Volkswagen bug and the Leica camera. It was scientifically designed to make the destroyed railroad track most difficult to repair.

As the German army retreated, the army engineers had also used high explosives to demolish the railroad's masonry bridges and pylons. This left long pieces of unsupported track dangling crazily in the air, like the one in this photo from January 1944, which shows a piece of track hanging unsupported over the demolished city of Ortona on the Adriatic shore. Note that there were no fishing boats to be seen on the calm blue Adriatic Sea.

I couldn't help thinking that Italians and Germans might have been far better off if they had stayed out of the Fascist Axis altogether. But I couldn't blame them for being bitter about the peace terms of World War I or for their desire to show the world that they could once again become a great world power.

> *At some level, I must have known that my mind would suppress these feelings and thereby preserve my sanity.*

while waiting. The tea water is boiling, desert style, in a well-blackened number ten can over a "desert stove" (right foreground). The stove is made of a cut-off flimsy tin with gasoline-soaked sand in the bottom.

At such a quiet moment, while waiting to go in with the infantry on a deadly assault, naturally our thoughts flowed to our own mortality, home, and Mother. The sonnet "To Mother" by Charles P. Edwards, from the "War Poems" chapter of his book *An AFS Driver Remembers,* speaks deeply hidden truth to me and stirs my own long-suppressed feelings about these events, the details of which I have still no memory at all. Perhaps that was why I took this photo. At some level, I must have known that my mind would suppress these feelings and thereby preserve my sanity.

I have no photographs and almost no memory of the battle of Monte Cassino. Presumably the things I witnessed were too horrible to be recalled. A shadowy memory flashed into my conscious mind recently when I re-read the poem "Cassino" by Charlie Edwards (on page 114). One line, "the Gurkhas at night with knives swinging" reminded me of a little haversack kit attached to a big Gurkha *kukri* knife in its battered and torn leather scabbard that I had found abandoned in the back of my ambulance after a busy night. I knew that no Gurkha soldier would ever voluntarily become separated from his *kukri,* and I had heard that when they died they would be buried with their knife, for religious reasons. The next morning, I went back to the hospital tent where I had delivered a severely wounded Gurkha solder the night before. They made good coffee, which I enjoyed with them, but they could find no record of such a patient having been admitted, nor could they find any record of what might have happened to his body, if he had been dead on arrival. So I kept the *kukri* and brought it home, mourning for him. It still makes me very uncomfortable even to think about that bloody knife.

Page 117
Near Ortona, Italy
Howard Brooke (with hat) had been evacuating patients at night without lights on a winding narrow mountain road near Ortona. (They did not use lights in order to avoid being spotted by the enemy.) He collided with a Sherman tank, also without lights, going in to support an air attack. The tank mashed the engine down, rode up on it and up and over Brooke's head, and rolled the ambulance over the bank. He and his patients could escape through the canvas roof, which had replaced the original metal roof, which had been crumpled by a previous rollover.

That night when he got back to our base, he breathed vigorously into my face and said loudly in a disturbed sort of barking voice, "I have just been run over by a Sherman tank, and I'm cold sober!"

Page 119
Near Ortona, Italy
After we returned from Cassino to San Vito on the Adriatic Coast, I was assigned to this Canadian first aid post. My ambulance is at the door to the first aid post, which is located for safety in the basement of this bombed-out brick building. Here, the wounded were stabilized for transport back to San Vito.

Note the temporary graves in the front yard and the overturned, blown-up German tank on the left side of the building. Even the trees could hardly survive the intense shelling and bombing of the battle for Ortona, which had lasted many months.

The mood of the Canadian medics at this first aid post was that of suspended animation; we lived a fearful suspended life, not knowing when the next war tragedy would strike.

When severely wounded were brought in, there was too much to be done. All hands leapt to their work

---

That night when he got back to our base, he breathed vigorously into my face and said loudly in a disturbed sort of barking voice, "I have just been run over by a Sherman tank, and I'm cold sober!"

---

with skill and vigor. But in those hours of long waiting, the presence of those graves in the front yard, and the dismal nature of the general scene, did get to us all.

One answer was the construction of a still, used for making a nasty-tasting liquor out of the green wine that could be found locally. When one man got really drunk, the doctor gave him a large intravenous dose of apomorphine, and just before the man stopped breathing, the doctor slapped his jaw violently while we held the man down. I was afraid it would break his jaw.

The man responded by projectile vomiting all over us, which is what the doctor intended. I never saw such a treatment before or since. That's one memory I can never forget!

Page 120
Casoli, Italy
The ancient castle of the noble di Ricci family is still intact at the top of the hill near Casoli, accessible only by long flights of stairs. The Baroness was an important person involved with civilian medical care. She invited me to lunch at the castle, where I met her husband the Baron and her lovely daughter, Francesca di Ricci. Francesca charmed us all but kept her distance. The di Ricci family had adopted a war

orphan baby boy and were raising him as their own. The di Ricci girls were much involved in taking care of him. That was an aspect of their family life that I never would have suspected until they invited me to the top of the castle to take photos.

Page 121
Casoli, Italy
My main duty with the Allied Military Government in Casoli, hill town of the upper Sangro, was to help Bob Read of the American Red Cross provide medical supplies for the Italian civilian hospital. They needed everything.

Page 122
Near Casoli, Italy
The soldiers of the reccy outfit were billeted in the old castle and in village homes. Soldiers and villagers lived and worked close together on top of this conical craggy hill, surrounded by snowy peaks and steep greening valleys. By day, we could watch the German soldiers at their posts across the valley. At night, they and the Indian soldiers would sneak down into the valley to lay booby traps and shoot at each other. In the morning, I would go down in my ambulance and pick up the wounded. It was a kind of game, but deadly serious. The front line had been stable here for months. The plan of the Allied armies appeared to be to keep the German army engaged here, in Italy, while preparations were being made to invade the coast of France.

Page 123
Civitella, Italy
I was assigned here to work with this Indian Army reconnaissance outfit. Soldiers of all ranks were friendly to me, especially Captain Ragaul, a Sikh, and Das, from Madras, assigned to me as my batman (servant). Captain Ragaul told me how frustrated he was that no matter how deserving he was, he could never be a commanding officer. Command of the Indian Army was always given to white British officers, no matter how stupid they were, or so it seemed to him.

Page 124
Civitella, Italy
At war so long, village women ignore ever-present Indian soldiers.

Page 125
Lama dei Peligni, Italy
I made home visits with Dr. Mario Cipolla, and was greatly impressed that he had stayed with his patients through the continual danger, the bombing, and the German demolition (scorched-earth policy). I did what little I could to help. He and the civilian guerilla fighters, the Patrioti, were the unsung heroes of this part of the war.

Page 126
Civitella, Italy
Coco, chief of the Patrioti guerillas, and his followers manned posts in the valleys below Civitella. They worked closely with the Indian Army reccy unit and later became an important force in clearing the Germans out of these mountains.

Page 127
Lama dei Peligni, Italy
These civilians from Lama dei Peligni, below Civitella, are bringing a stretcher case to my ambulance.

Page 128
Mid-Atlantic Ocean
I am about to be transferred from the Liberty ship *Henry Wadsworth Longfellow* to the destroyer escort alongside in order to have the Navy doctor reduce my dislocated shoulder. In our joy to be going home at the end of our term of AFS service, we were celebrating by playing leapfrog on deck. When the ship lurched, I caught my hand under a hatch-cover strap and fell forward, causing the dislocation.

WAR POEMS AND AFS HISTORY

Charles Pastene Edwards, "The Fox"–Lifelong Friend, Pacifist and Poet

eyes bright and mind sharp

his words of wisdom bubbled

like a mountain brook

Over the past seventy years, Charlie Edwards and I have been friends, following each other around the world. We were in the same class in elementary and high school at Milton Academy; worked together on a Quaker work project draining a malaria swamp in the jungle of Paso de Ovejas, Vera Cruz, Mexico; sailed together on the troopship *Aquitania* from New York to Port Tewfik, Egypt; and were together in Selemiye, Syria, and also during much of the North African and Italian campaigns as volunteer AFS ambulance drivers, serving the British Eighth Army in the same AFS platoon and sometimes the same ambulance. We kept up with each other after the war through frequent reunions of the AFS and an active correspondence by mail, especially about his book An AFS Driver Remembers, which was privately printed and included many of my photographs and letters home.

Following are Charlie's thoughts about war, peace, and poetry.

War is the most destructive of human enterprises; and yet war summons sacrifice, and demands creative endeavor. In the crucible of total war, our scientists unleashed a force capable of destroying life on the planet, but also harnessed atomic energy for peaceful purposes. Out of the agony of war, statesmen promise a "new world order." And as we search for just peace, we ponder the absence, in time of peace, of the moral equivalent to the sacrifices that war commands.

Swept as I was with my generation into the maelstrom of World War II, I was authorized under Selective Service for combat medical duty from 1942 to 1945 with the American (Ambulance) Field Service (AFS), assigned to British army units in the Mideast, North Africa, and Italy. Several of my poems based on these experiences are included in Fragments of Peace.

"Battlefield Cross," a sonnet, describes a crude cross placed beside a blown-out tank to mark a temporary battlefield grave in Italy in November 1943. In "To Mother," also a sonnet, I imagine my own battlefield grave. "No Place for Kids" and "Preb" honor the memory of two comrades-in-arms, one wounded near Ortona, Italy, in January 1944 and the other killed in action on November 28, 1943, during our advance against the German armies in Italy. Preb's ambulance was the first ambulance across the Sangro River.

I wrote "These Four Walls" after a brutal German barrage at Enfidaville, Tunisia, in May 1943. I served there for three weeks at a frontline regimental aid post with a light field artillery regiment of the British Eighth Army. The final remnant of Rommel's Afrika Korps surrendered through our lines.

In February 1944, I witnessed at first hand the destruction of the famous Abbey at Monte Cassino following the annihilation of the city of Cassino itself, and I wrote the poem "Cassino." This poem and the five that preceded it honor the bravery of the soldier and the supreme sacrifice made by many, but they also document the horror and brutality of modern war. Man is Destroyer, even when waging a "just war" for the cause of freedom against an aggressor.

In 1984 I returned to Cassino, and I was dumbfounded to find the Abbey arisen phoenixlike upon its mountain, and the city no less marvelously restored. Thus inspired, I wrote the poem "Monte Cassino Revisited." It represents my hopes for the triumph of Man the Creator, and for the ultimate victory of peace over war.

MONTE CASSINO REVISITED, 1984

Charles P. Edwards

The mild, sweet Saint,
his sister sanctified
together built
where the rude Goths had trod,
a shrine to peace
and a path
to God

Where the mountain rose
straight from the valley floor
the shining Abbey stood upon its peak,
a beacon for a darkened world.

Toppled by man's militant hand,
rebuilt, destroyed, again rebuilt
brick upon single brick, stone upon
   stone, until

caught in the vise of world-wide war,
attacked from air and ground,
its golden crypt, its marble halls
blasted to dust.
Nothing remained but sightless craters
   filled
with croaking frogs.
The Abbey and its town below
   were stilled.

Today transformed
the snow-white Abbey crowns its
   mountain home,
proudly proclaims PAX as pilgrims come
from every shore,
bears witness to the Saint's eternal dream
that peace will conquer war.

ON THE BEACH — ORTONA

Charles P. Edwards, © 2001

Canadian Military Cemetery, Ortona, Italy

On the bluff above
where winds the Moro River
to the sea,
a thousand young men sleep
where they must forever be.

Far below
a thousand gay umbrellas
on the beach
shelter a holiday throng
careless and free.

Row on row the headstones march
as if on parade:
young lives sacrificed
to right the shame
of all who lit the flame
of war and holocaust.

Each star or cross
bears a name
with words etched in stone
to represent
a Mother's moan,
a lover's cry:
a Father's agony
"My love, my son
beautiful beyond compare
your loss too terrible
for me
to bear."

Life for them
will never be
the same, and he
will not come home again.
The new world
called upon
to give the old
a second chance;
will such sacrifice,
such pain,
be all in vain?

Play on
festive throng
upon your beach
careless and free,
thanks to these
immortal dead
for yet another day.

Until the old world
and the new
together seek
and reach the way
to Peace on Earth,
the winds of war
too soon
will build and blow
your lovely beach
away.

WAVES OF TOLERANCE (SONNET FOR THE DESERT WAR)

Jock Cobb, 1943 and 2010

As dawn spreads up the sky, and stars fade away,
Zephyr's gentle breezes start the desert day
Wafting waves of tolerance onto desert shores
Easing malice left from yesterday's mad wars.

Where Space seduces Time, and Sand is all,
When battles back and forth boom and fall
With neither army winning much at all,
Great thoughts are springing up among the small:

Our foes have hopes and feelings, and we the same.
We're fighting for the peacetime, not hatred's flame.
Our human souls have echoed that war's a scam.
We're all warmonger victims in a Ponzi game.

Unless Mankind could stop this profiteering wrong,
Humans might keep fighting 'til all the men were gone.

AMERICAN FIELD SERVICE HISTORY

When I was in my late teens, I was lucky to be part of the Experiment in International Living, a program started in 1932 by a Quaker named Donald B. Watt. As one of the early "experimenters," I studied and lived with a family in France in 1936. A decade later, I was among former AFS ambulance driver volunteers who participated in the birth of another similar program.

The AFS, or American Field Service (originally the American Ambulance Field Service), had its origins early in the twentieth century. It was started as a volunteer ambulance service in France in 1914 by A. Platt Andrew and was developed and coordinated by Stephen Galatti.

The son of Greek immigrants, Galatti graduated from Harvard in 1910 and volunteered as an ambulance driver in 1915. After a year in Alsace, he became assistant inspector general of the AFS, moved to Paris, and spearheaded the whole AFS operation. He was hardworking and a gifted organizer, a warm and dedicated person, a friend to everyone who worked with him. The AFS had a special esprit right from the start.

After World War I, Galatti worked in New York City as a banker and stockbroker, continuing to volunteer time and energy with the AFS in a fellowship program that a group of AFS drivers had started. They worked with the Institute of International Education to provide scholarships for American university students to do graduate studies in France.

At the outbreak of World War II in 1939, Steve Galatti reactivated the AFS ambulance service and, as its director general, provided ambulances and volunteers for the Allied armies. AFS units deployed some 2,196 men and 427 ambulances, all donated or acquired under Lend-Lease arrangements, providing a major portion of the frontline ambulance service for British and Allied forces in France, Syria, North Africa, Italy, Germany, and the India-Burma theaters.

With the end of World War II, Galatti and the AFS Board of Directors saw a new opportunity to make an important contribution to world peace through AFS International Scholarships, a student exchange program for high school students. The first group of students brought to the United States to live for a year with American families came from ten countries:

The American Field Service believes in youth—in its ability to see clearly, to see through the fog of propaganda, to see with the eyes of the heart.

—Steve Galatti

Czechoslovakia, Estonia, France, Great Britain, Greece, Hungary, the Netherlands, New Zealand, Norway, and Syria. Soon American students were living and studying abroad as well—with families that had felt the ravages of war and perhaps even lost a child to war, or with families that valued peace so much that to advance its cause, they would gladly share their love, hearth, and home with a foreign exchange student. Holly, my wife, was the first corresponding secretary for the AFS Student Exchange Office in Boston during 1947–1948 while she was pregnant with our first son, Loren.

By the time Galatti died in 1964, AFS had exchange programs in sixty countries. Now the AFS International Cultural Exchange arranges more than ten thousand student exchanges each year, about 60 percent of them exchanges between countries other than the United States. The AFS has become a truly international organization with about fifty actively coordinating independent regional centers all over the world. AFS International has one hundred thousand volunteers worldwide who work with the schools, families, and students in their communities to help develop knowledge, skills, and understanding and to create a more just and peaceful world. The AFS esprit continues.

A DIFFERENT ROAD MAP FOR WORLD PEACE

Jock Cobb, 2009

Worldwide peace would gain a valid stand
If ten million students could arrange
to join an intercultural exchange
and travel for a study year abroad.

They'd live with families in a foreign land
and study at a local (foreign) school;
so they would learn to speak the local tongue,
make friends, and share in family chores and fun.

This should bring the world to understand
the truth so many frontline medics saw
while sharing woes and fears and hopes and fate
with other frontline soldiers in the war:
In spite of different language, faith, or skin,
deep at heart, all humans are akin.

Every gun that is made, every warship launched, every rocket fired
signifies, in the final sense, a theft from those who hunger and
are not fed, those who are cold and are not clothed. This
world in arms is not spending money alone. It is
spending the sweat of its laborers, the genius
of its scientists, the hopes of its children.
This is not a way of life at all in any
true sense. Under the cloud
of threatening war, it is
humanity hanging
from a cross
of iron.

—Dwight D. Eisenhower
*from a speech before the American Society of
Newspaper Editors, April 16, 1953*

World War II was the deadliest military conflict in history. The
twentieth-century hemoclysm left 50 to 70 million dead:
40 to 52 million civilians.
22 to 25 million military.
13 to 20 million due to war-related disease and famine.
5 million prisoners of war.